Two Boys

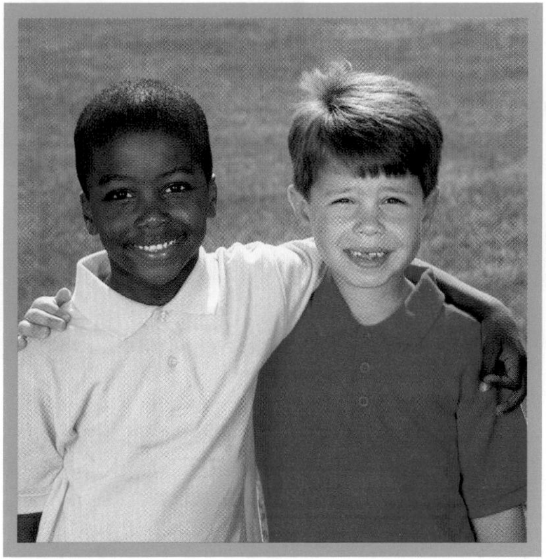

Written by Judy Nayer
Photographs by John Paul Endress

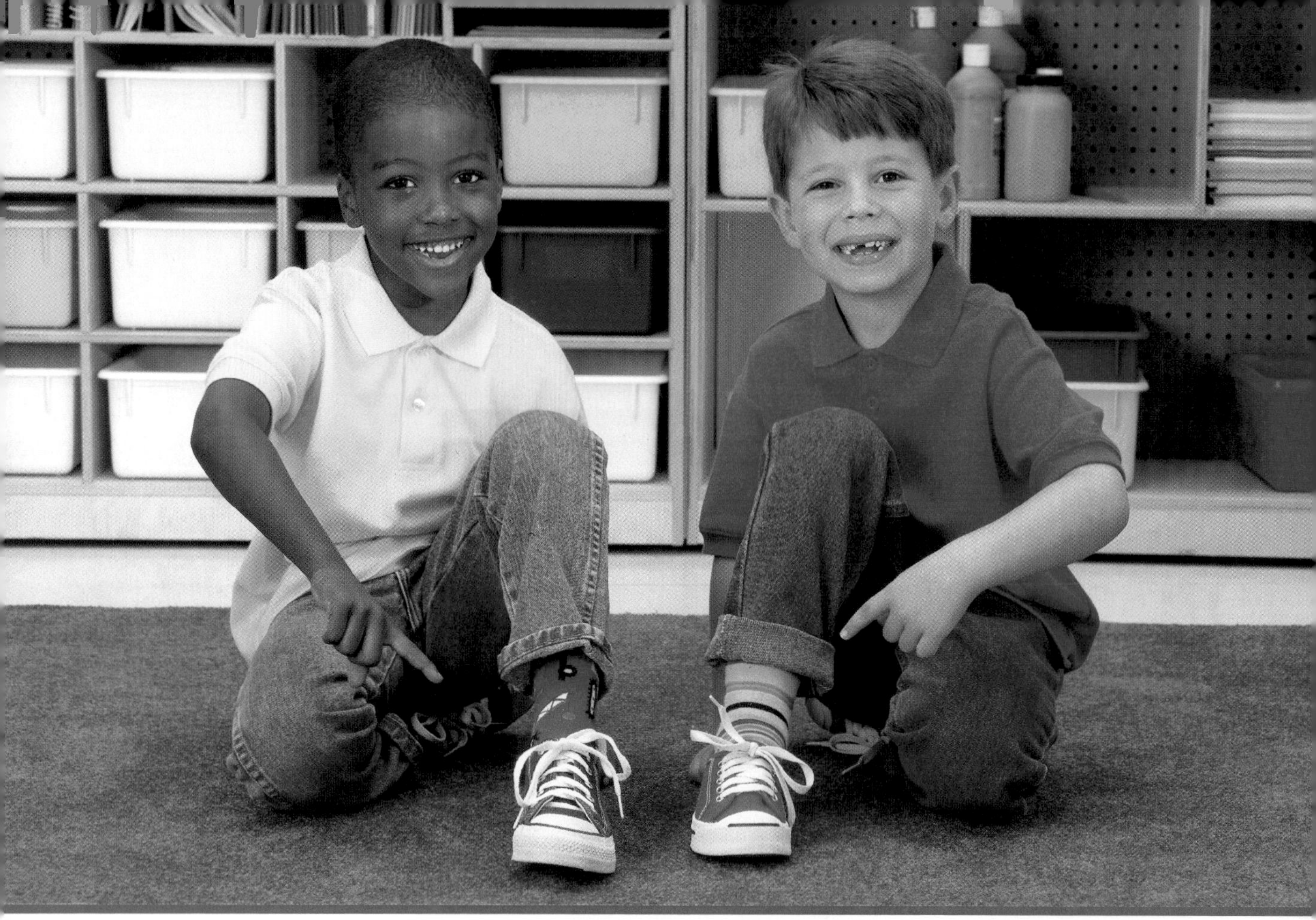

Two socks.

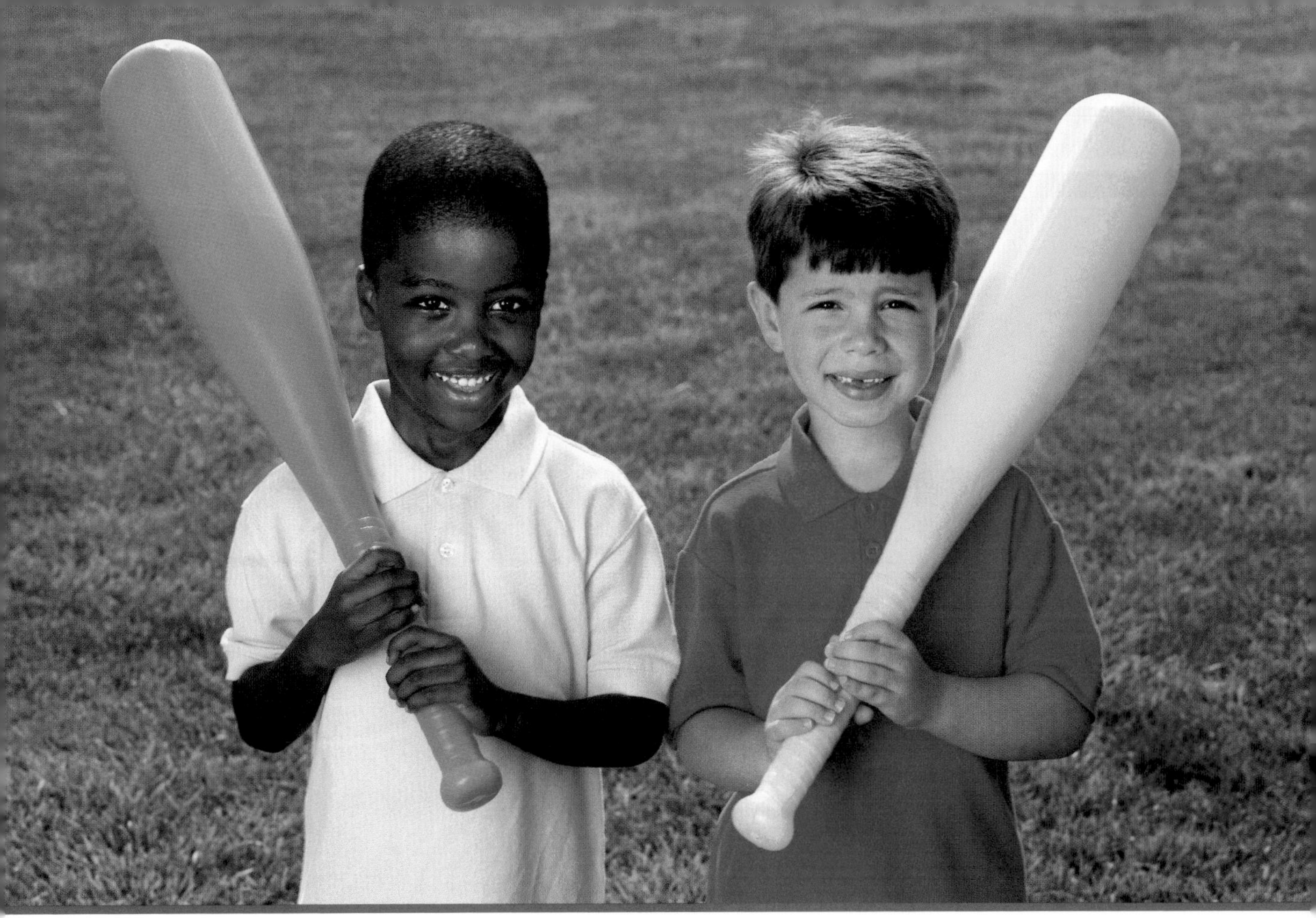

Two bats.

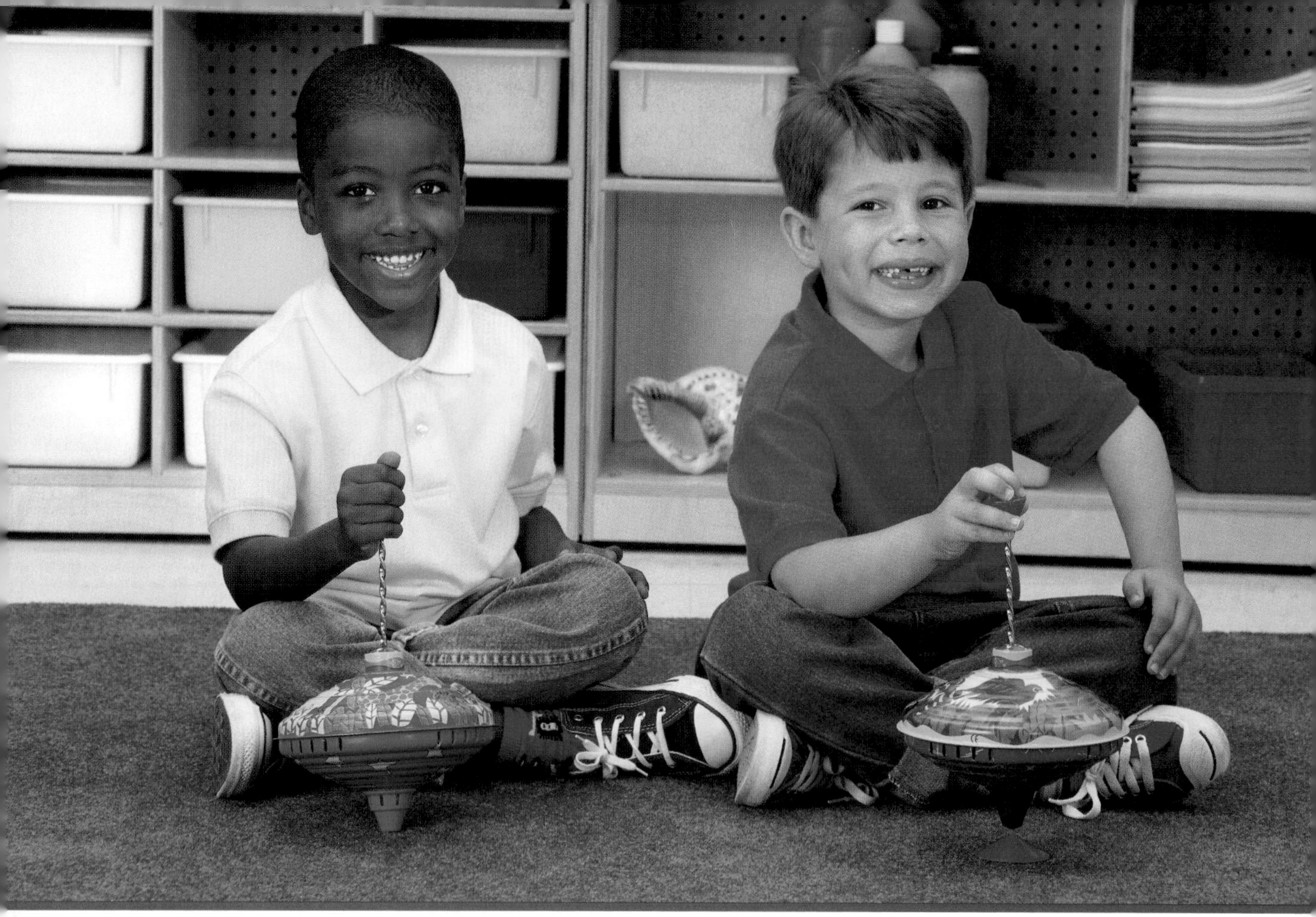

Two tops.

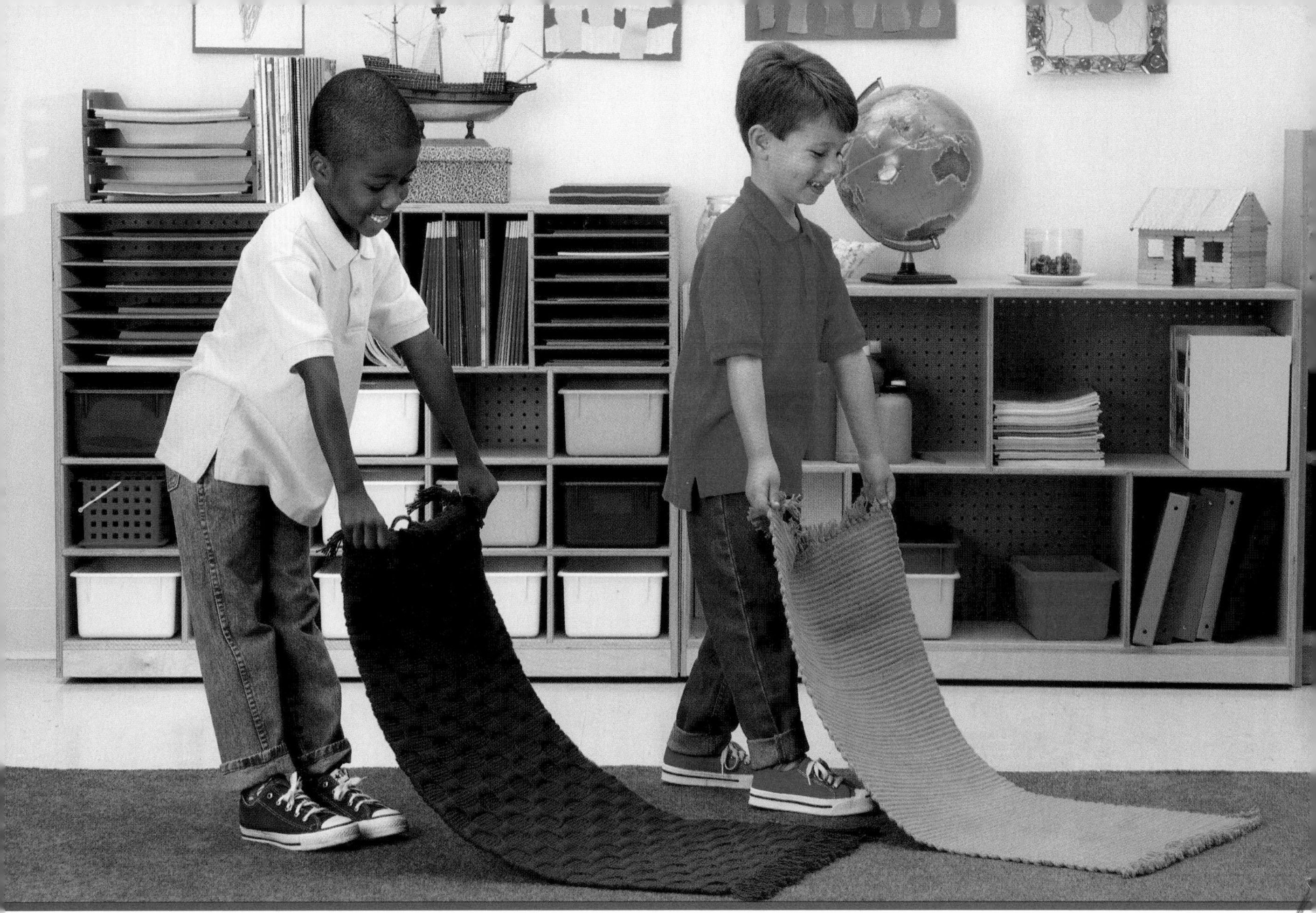

Two mats.

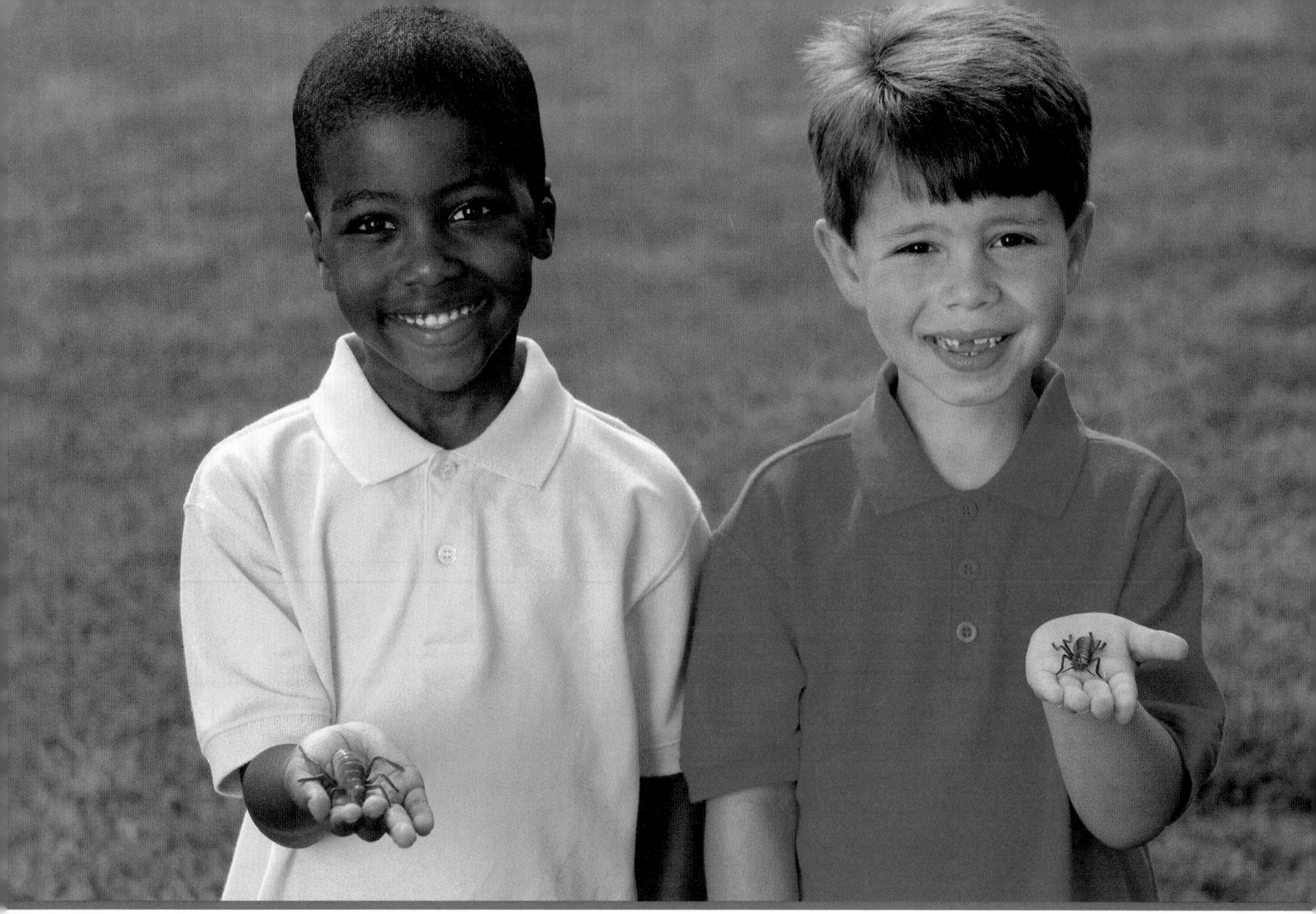

Two bugs.

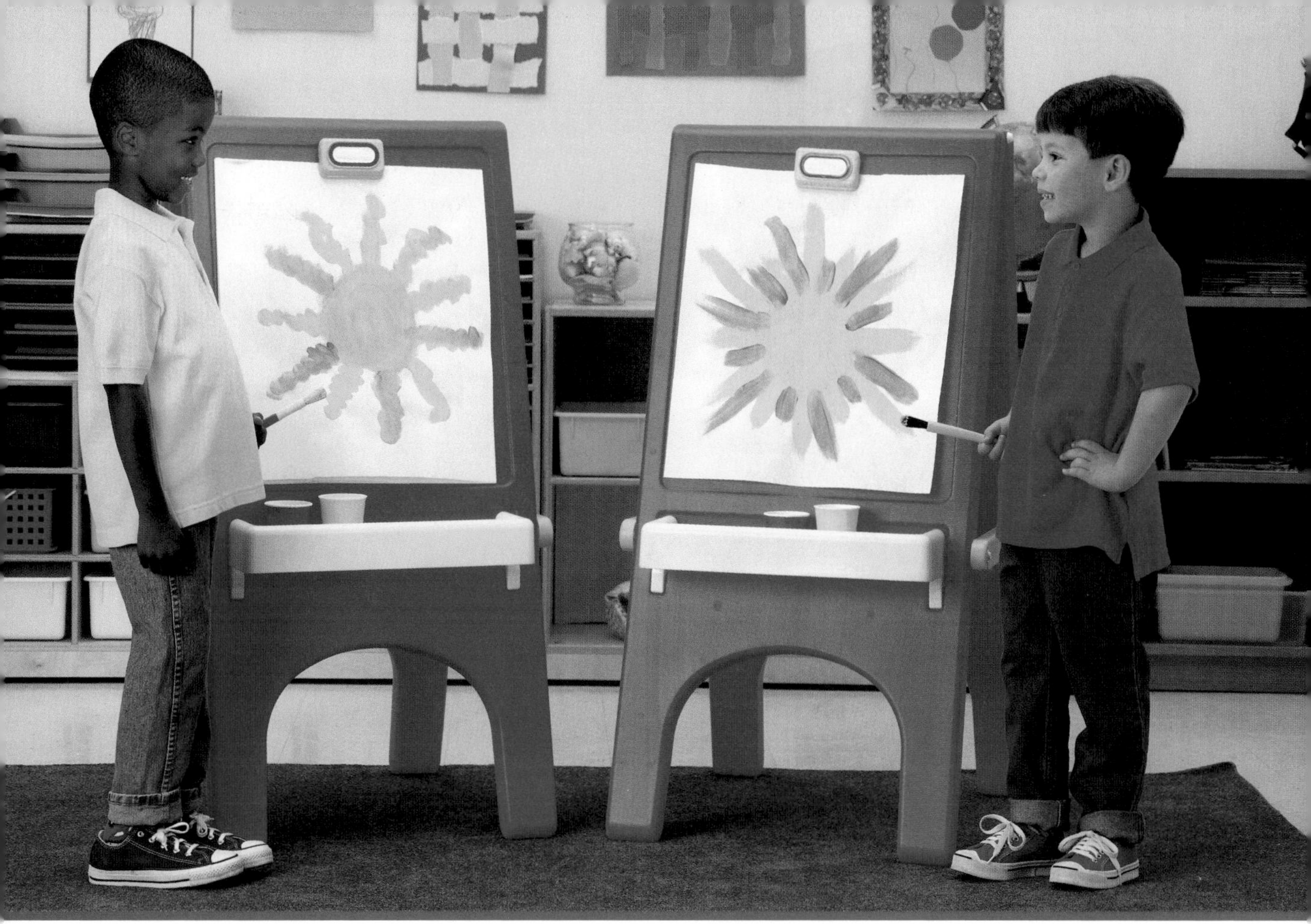

Two suns.

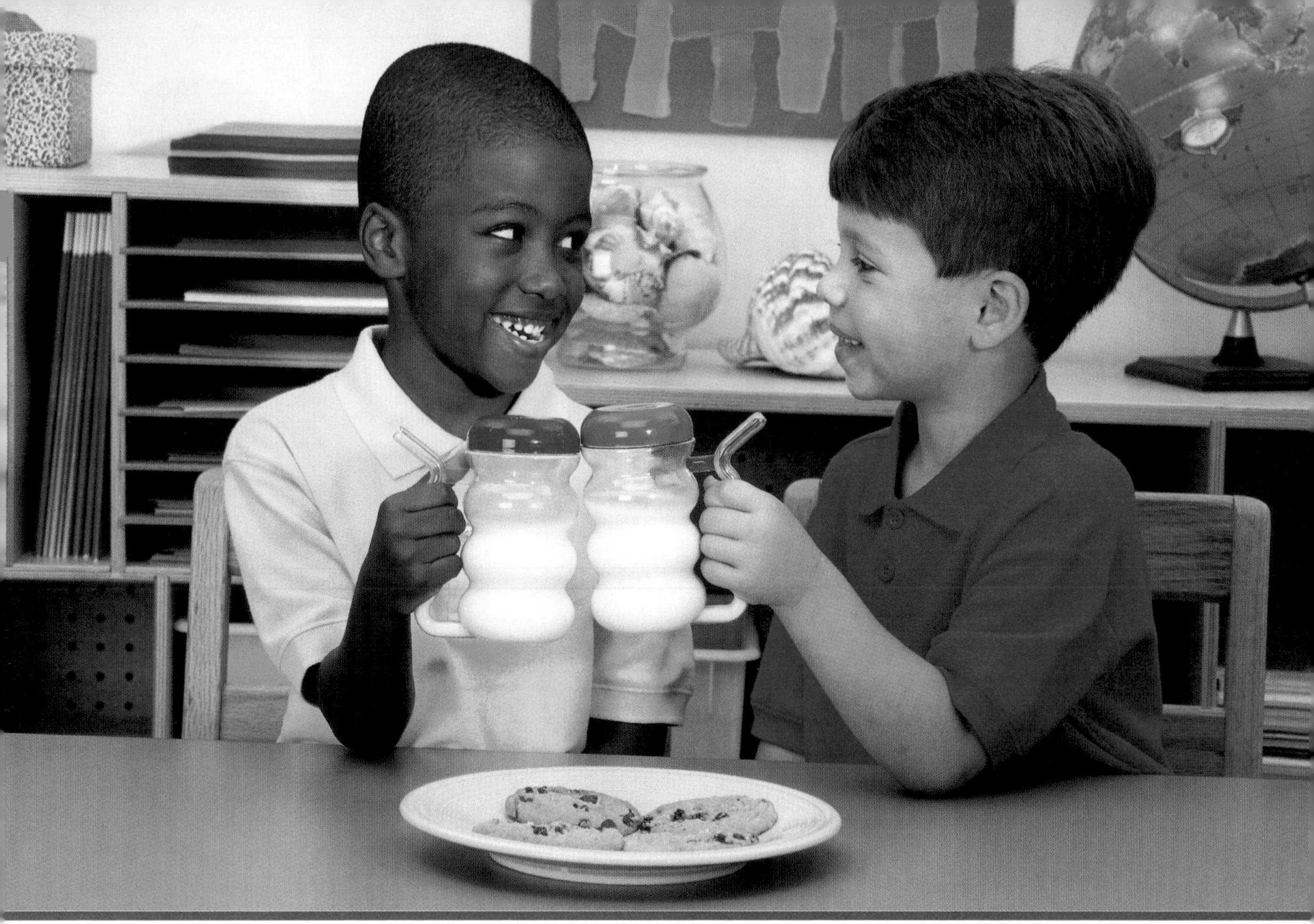

Two friends.